LORD, SEND ME

I0145022

PASTOR DR. CLAUDINE BENJAMIN

Published by:

Editor: Cleveland O. McLeish (Author C. Orville McLeish)

ISBN: 978-1-965635-48-3 (paperback)

DEDICATION

To every willing vessel who has ever said, "Yes, Lord."

This book is for the laborers who have answered the call and those who are still wrestling with the weight of it. May your obedience become someone else's salvation.

To the One who called me, shaped me, and still sends me—my Lord and Savior, Jesus Christ—this book is for You. You found me when I was unqualified, You anointed me when I felt unworthy, and You sent me when I had no map but Your voice. Every word on these pages is an echo of my obedience to Your call. May You receive all the glory, now and forever.

To the soul winners, the missionaries, the street preachers, the altar workers, and the intercessors who labor in quiet places, unknown to man but celebrated in heaven—this is for you. You said yes when it was costly. You stayed when it was painful. You went when others remained. May you be strengthened and reminded: Your work is not in vain **(see 1 Corinthians 15:58).**

To the next generation of sent ones, the called, the compelled, the burning hearts waiting for direction—I see you, and heaven sees you. May this book be a blueprint for your obedience, a torch to ignite your passion, and a confirmation of the fire God has placed inside you. The world is waiting for your "yes."

To every pastor, leader, and believer who has ever prayed, "Lord, send me"—this is a witness that God still sends, still speaks, and still uses those who will surrender. You don't have to be famous, flawless, or favored by man—just faithful.

Finally, to those I've loved and led, to those I've prayed for and wept over, to those I've been sent to reach—you are the reason I keep saying yes.

This book is for the sent.

Now go—and don't come back empty-handed.

—Pastor Claudine Benjamin

ACKNOWLEDGMENT

I want to first acknowledge my Lord and Savior, Jesus Christ, who called me, equipped me, and sent me—not because I was perfect, but because I was willing.

To my family, friends, mentors, and spiritual leaders, thank you for nurturing the gift within me.

To every soul winner, intercessor, and missionary: your work is not in vain (**see 1 Corinthians 15:58**).

To the reader—thank you for accepting the challenge to say, "Lord, send me."

ABOUT THE AUTHOR

Pastor Claudine Benjamin is a passionate preacher, teacher, and intercessor who has dedicated her life to fulfilling the Great Commission and equipping the Body of Christ to walk in bold obedience. With a heart that burns for evangelism and revival, she carries a prophetic mantle that calls the church back to its original assignment: to go out, reach the lost, and make disciples of all nations.

A seasoned ministry leader and compassionate shepherd, Pastor Claudine has spent years mentoring believers, raising up soul-winners, and ministering healing and restoration to the broken. Her messages are marked by urgency, truth, and the power of the Holy Spirit, awakening a generation to surrender to God's divine calling.

Lord, Send Me is a personal cry and a divine mandate—an invitation to the reader to step out of comfort and into commission. Pastor Claudine's writing flows from a deep well of scripture, real-life experience, and unwavering faith in the God who still calls, equips, and sends.

She continues to speak in churches, conferences, and evangelistic events, encouraging believers to live lives of obedience, prayer, and action. When she's not preaching or writing, she's mentoring young leaders, serving in her local church, and spending time in God's presence.

Pastor Claudine Benjamin is also the author of numerous books and resources aimed at spiritual growth, healing, and purpose-driven living. Her mission remains clear: to see lives transformed, souls saved, and God's glory revealed in the earth.

TABLE OF CONTENTS

CHAPTER 1

THE CALL STILL STANDS

The call to be sent by God is not a historical concept reserved for prophets of old, apostles of the early church, or missionaries of the past. It is a present, urgent, and divine summons that still echoes through the hearts of men and women today. God is still calling. The question is: Are we still listening?

God's Call Is Eternal

In Isaiah 6, we read the powerful moment where the prophet hears the voice of the Lord:

> **"Also I heard the voice of the Lord, saying: 'Whom shall I send, and who will go for Us?' Then said I, 'Here am I! Send me.'" —Isaiah 6:8 (NKJV)**

This divine inquiry was not due to God's lack of ability, but rather His desire to partner with willing vessels. Isaiah's response should not be viewed as an isolated historical moment, but as a prototype of what God desires from every believer today. His call did not end in the Old Testament, nor did it expire with the apostles. The call still stands.

Jesus confirmed this in the New Testament when He gave the Great Commission:

> **"Go therefore and make disciples of all the nations, baptizing them in the name of the Father and of the Son and of the Holy Spirit." —Matthew 28:19 (NKJV)**

The word "go" is not a suggestion—it is a command. And it still applies.

The Problem Is Not the Call—It's the Response

God has always had a message and a mission, but He looks for messengers. In every generation, the harvest is plentiful, but the laborers remain few (**see Matthew 9:37**). It's not because the call has weakened, but because the response has diminished. Distractions, fear, comfort, and personal ambition have drowned out the sound of God's voice.

We see this again in Romans:

> **"For the gifts and the calling of God are irrevocable." — Romans 11:29 (ESV)**

God does not retract His call. He doesn't change His mind. The same God who called Abraham to leave his country, who called Moses from the burning bush, who called Paul on the Damascus road, is calling us now.

God Still Uses Ordinary People

There's a dangerous myth that the "called" must be flawless, educated, and charismatic. But God has always used the unlikely:

- Moses had a stutter.
- David was a shepherd boy.
- Jeremiah thought he was too young.
- Peter was impulsive.
- Paul was a former persecutor.

None of them were perfect, but they were called.

> **"But God has chosen the foolish things of the world to put to shame the wise... that no flesh should glory in His presence." —1 Corinthians 1:27, 29 (NKJV)**

The call of God is not about your qualifications—it's about your willingness.

Reviving the Cry: 'Here Am I!'

The words "Here am I, send me" must become more than a Sunday morning lyric or a missionary slogan. It must be the cry of the surrendered heart. This generation does not lack purpose—it lacks surrender. The altar of God has too often been replaced with stages of performance or platforms of popularity. But the call of God requires laying down your agenda to pick up His.

> **"Then He said to them all, 'If anyone desires to come after Me, let him deny himself, and take up his cross daily, and follow Me.'" —Luke 9:23 (NKJV)**

True sending requires true sacrifice. God sends those who are dead to self and alive to His Spirit.

The Call Is Both Personal and Global

God calls us individually, but never just for ourselves. Isaiah's personal encounter led to a public commission. The same is true today. You may be called to your family, community, nation, or the nations of the earth; wherever you're called, your voice, feet, and obedience matter.

> **"How then shall they call on Him in whom they have not believed? And how shall they believe in Him of whom they have not heard? And how shall they hear without a preacher?" —Romans 10:14 (NKJV)**

Someone is waiting on the other side of your "yes."

The Invitation Still Stands

The call of God still rings. It is persistent. It is holy. It is weighty. But it is also beautiful. You are not too young, too old, too broken, or too late. If you can still hear His voice, you can still answer.

Will you respond like Isaiah? Will you lift your hands, your heart, and your life and say, "Lord, send me"?

REFLECTION QUESTIONS

1. Have you heard the call of God in your own life? If so, how have you responded?

2. What are some personal distractions or fears that have hindered your response?

3. In what ways can you be more surrendered to God's mission in this season?

DECLARATION

I am chosen, called, and commissioned by God. I will not ignore His voice. I say yes to His will and His way. I am not afraid to go, for I am sent by the King of kings. Lord, send me!

CHAPTER 2

A WILLING VESSEL

God does not need our strength—He needs our surrender. The power to do great exploits for the kingdom does not begin with our ability, but with our availability. While many seek to be qualified, God seeks those who are simply willing. The question has never been, "Can God use me?" The real question is, "Will I let Him?"

The Power of Willingness

In 2 Timothy, the apostle Paul speaks of vessels:

> **"Therefore if anyone cleanses himself from the latter, he will be a vessel for honor, sanctified and useful for the Master, prepared for every good work." —2 Timothy 2:21 (NKJV)**

The emphasis is not on the external appearance of the vessel, but on its usefulness to the Master. The most beautiful cup that refuses to be filled is of no use to the thirsty. In the same way, God looks for those who may not have it all together, but who are willing to be poured into, and poured out.

God Chooses the Available Over the Able

When God called Gideon, he was hiding in fear (**see Judges 6:11**). When He called Moses, Moses questioned his own speech (**see Exodus 4:10**). Yet God still used them because they made themselves available.

> **"Then Moses said to the Lord, "O my Lord, I am not eloquent, neither before nor since You have spoken to Your servant; but I am slow of speech and slow of tongue." So the Lord said to him, "Who has made man's mouth? Or who makes the mute, the deaf, the seeing, or the blind? Have not I, the Lord?" —Exodus 4:10–11 (NKJV)**

This interaction reveals something powerful: God isn't impressed by our resumes. He's moved by our "yes."

The Heart That Says, "Use Me, Lord"

David, the shepherd boy turned king, was not chosen because of stature, but because of heart:

> **"For the Lord does not see as man sees; for man looks at the outward appearance, but the Lord looks at the heart." —1 Samuel 16:7 (NKJV)**

This is the heart of a willing vessel:

- Humble
- Teachable
- Available
- Dependent on God

When God finds a heart like that, He entrusts His assignments.

Willingness Requires Obedience

It is one thing to say, "Lord, use me." It is another thing to obey when He gives instructions. Willingness is tested not in convenience, but in obedience.

> **"If you are willing and obedient, you shall eat the good of the land." —Isaiah 1:19 (NKJV)**

Obedience is the evidence of true willingness. God told Abraham to leave his country, not knowing where he was going (**see Genesis 12:1**). Abraham obeyed God's command. Willing vessels do not always have the full picture, but they trust the One giving the directions.

Broken but Willing

Some believe their past disqualifies them. But scripture reveals a pattern: God uses broken people who are willing to be made whole.

- Rahab had a reputation, but was willing to hide the spies (**see Joshua 2**).
- Jonah ran, but when he yielded, an entire city repented (**see Jonah 3**).
- Peter denied Christ, but later preached, and 3,000 were saved (**see Acts 2:41**).

Your brokenness is not the issue. Your unwillingness is. God is not looking for perfection—He's looking for surrender.

Willingness Opens the Door to Miracles

When Jesus turned water into wine at the wedding in Cana, the servants played a key role:

> **"Jesus said to them, 'Fill the waterpots with water.' And they filled them up to the brim." —John 2:7 (NKJV)**

They obeyed without question. That act of simple willingness triggered a miracle. Many want God to move, but few are willing to move with Him.

Say Yes Before You Know the Details

God often gives the assignment before He gives the full explanation. Willing vessels do not wait for all the answers—they respond in faith.

> **"Trust in the Lord with all your heart, and lean not on your own understanding; in all your ways acknowledge Him, and He shall direct your paths." —Proverbs 3:5–6 (NKJV)**

Saying "yes" to God means walking by faith, not by sight. It means giving Him your schedule, plans, and limitations, and trusting Him to use it all for His glory.

The Vessel Is You

God is still seeking vessels. Not perfect ones. Not polished ones. Just willing ones. If you're reading this, it's because God is stirring your heart to be used for something greater than yourself. He asks, "Will you go?" and waits for your answer.

You don't have to have it all figured out. You just need to be empty enough to be filled and humble enough to be used.

REFLECTION QUESTIONS

1. Have you been hesitant to say "yes" to God because of fear or feelings of inadequacy?

2. What areas of your life do you need to surrender in order to be a willing vessel?

3. What is one step you can take today to become more available to God's calling?

DECLARATION

I am a vessel for the Master's use. Though I may be imperfect, I am willing. I surrender my plans for His purpose. Lord, I say yes—use me for Your glory.

CHAPTER 3

HEARING THE VOICE OF GOD

Before a person can be sent, they must first hear. Every divine assignment begins with divine instruction. One of the greatest hindrances to fulfilling the call of God is not rebellion—it's misdirection due to spiritual deafness. The Lord is always speaking, but are we truly listening?

> **"My sheep hear My voice, and I know them, and they follow Me." —John 10:27 (NKJV)**

Hearing God's voice is not reserved for prophets or pastors—it is the birthright of every believer who belongs to the Shepherd. To be a vessel that God sends, we must first be people who know how to discern His voice.

God Still Speaks

From Genesis to Revelation, God has been a speaking God. He spoke to Adam in the garden (**see Genesis 3**), to Noah about the ark (**see Genesis 6**), to Moses through a burning bush (**see Exodus 3**), and to Samuel in the temple (**see 1 Samuel 3**). He spoke through visions, dreams, angels, prophets, and most powerfully through His Son, Jesus Christ (**see Hebrews 1:1-2**).

That same God still speaks today.

"He who has an ear, let him hear what the Spirit says to the churches." —Revelation 3:22 (NKJV)

The Holy Spirit, who lives within believers, is not mute. He convicts, leads, warns, instructs, and reveals truth.

How God Speaks Today

1. **Through the Word** – The Bible is God's written voice. It is alive and relevant.

   "All Scripture is given by inspiration of God..." —2 Timothy 3:16 (NKJV)

If you want to sharpen your spiritual hearing, start by immersing yourself in His Word. The more scripture you hide in your heart, the more familiar His voice becomes.

2. **Through the Holy Spirit** – The Spirit bears witness with our spirit.

   "The Spirit Himself bears witness with our spirit that we are children of God." —Romans 8:16 (NKJV)

He nudges, speaks in stillness, gives peace or discomfort, and reminds us of Christ's teachings.

3. **Through Prayer** – Prayer is not a monologue but a dialogue.

   "Call to Me, and I will answer you, and show you great

and mighty things…" —Jeremiah 33:3 (NKJV)

In moments of prayer, clarity is born.

4. **Through Peace or Lack Thereof** – God often confirms His will through peace.

   "Let the peace of God rule in your hearts…" — Colossians 3:15 (NKJV)

When peace departs, it's often a sign that we are out of step with His will.

5. **Through Godly Counsel** – Wise, Spirit-filled believers may confirm what God is already speaking.

   "In the multitude of counselors there is safety." — Proverbs 11:14 (NKJV)

6. **Through Circumstances** – While we must be cautious not to base doctrine on experience, God can close and open doors to redirect us (**see Revelation 3:7-8**).

Obstacles to Hearing God's Voice

While God is always speaking, we are not always postured to hear. Here are several reasons people struggle to hear Him:

- **Noise:** The world is loud. Social media, entertainment, and opinions often drown out the whisper of the Holy Spirit.

- **Sin:** Sin dulls spiritual senses.

  "But your iniquities have separated you from your God..." —Isaiah 59:2 (NKJV)

- **Disobedience:** Repeated disobedience can harden the heart.

  "Today, if you will hear His voice, do not harden your hearts..." —Hebrews 3:15 (NKJV)

- **Impatience:** Some miss God's voice because they won't wait.

  "Be still, and know that I am God." —Psalm 46:10 (NKJV)

- **Doubt:** When people do not believe He will speak, they tune out the possibility of divine communication.

  "But let him ask in faith, with no doubting..." —James 1:6 (NKJV)

Developing a Listening Heart

The prophet Samuel learned to hear God in the stillness of the night.

"Speak, for Your servant hears." —1 Samuel 3:10 (NKJV)

This must be the posture of every believer who desires to be sent: a servant who listens. Cultivating a life that hears God means:

- Creating regular quiet time.
- Asking God to speak.
- Journaling what you believe He says.
- Comparing impressions with scripture.
- Submitting personal revelation to spiritual leadership when needed.

Hearing Prepares You to Be Sent

Before Jesus sent out His disciples, He spent time teaching and speaking to them. They learned His voice in private before they represented Him in public.

"Then He appointed twelve, that they might be with Him and that He might send them out to preach." —Mark 3:14 (NASB)

To be sent, you must first sit. Time in God's presence sharpens your spiritual senses and strengthens your spiritual confidence.

Listen Before You Leap

Many leap into ministry, decisions, or missions without listening to the Lord. But to be effective, you must first be informed. God is still calling. But He does not shout over noise—He speaks to those who lean in.

"The Lord God has given Me the tongue of the learned... He awakens Me morning by morning, He awakens My ear to hear as the learned." —Isaiah 50:4 (NKJV)

He desires to awaken your ears. He wants to walk with you, speak to you, and lead you before He sends you. Because only those who hear can declare, and only those who know His voice can carry His message.

REFLECTION QUESTIONS

1. Are there areas in your life that are too loud for you to hear God clearly?

2. What intentional steps can you take to grow more sensitive to His voice?

3. Can you recall a time when you ignored God's voice? What was the result?

DECLARATION

Lord, I quiet my soul to hear Your voice. I will not move unless You speak. I am Your servant—speak to me, lead me, and send me. I declare that I walk in step with the Spirit, and I will obey what You say.

CHAPTER 4

WHAT IT REALLY MEANS TO BE SENT

Being "sent" by God is not a poetic phrase or a religious slogan—it is a divine commission, a kingdom assignment, and a spiritual responsibility. To be sent by God is to be deputized by heaven to carry out a mission on earth. It is not about title, popularity, or applause—it's about obedience, sacrifice, and eternal impact.

> **"So Jesus said to them again, "Peace to you! As the Father has sent Me, I also send you."" —John 20:21 (NKJV)**

To be sent means to represent someone higher. Jesus was sent by the Father. Now we are sent by Christ. Therefore, our sending is sacred.

Sent Ones Are Not Self-Appointed

True sending begins with a call and a commission. In today's culture, many move prematurely, not because God sent them, but because they sent themselves. But divine sending is not driven by ambition; it is birthed in the secret place.

> **"And no man takes this honor to himself, but he who is called by God, just as Aaron was." —Hebrews 5:4 (NKJV)**

God does not honor unauthorized assignments. Those who are sent carry both authority and accountability.

The Sent Life Requires a Shift

To be sent is to:

- Surrender your personal plans.
- Embrace divine instructions.
- Be willing to go wherever, whenever, and however God leads.

> **"Then I said, 'Here am I! Send me.' And He said, 'Go, and tell this people...'" —Isaiah 6:8–9 (NKJV)**

Isaiah's call did not end with his "yes." God immediately gave him direction. Saying yes to being sent means accepting what comes after the yes—hard places, hard people, and holy purpose.

Being Sent Requires Walking in God's Timing

God's sending is strategic. He sends you to the right place, at the right time, with the right message. Consider Jesus' instructions to the disciples:

> **"Do not go into the way of the Gentiles... But go rather to the lost sheep of the house of Israel." —Matthew 10:5–6 (NKJV)**

Even Jesus' sending had specific instructions. If you're truly sent, you move when God says move, not when doors look open or opportunities look exciting.

God's timing protects you, positions you, and produces lasting fruit.

The Sent Must Be Prepared to Be Rejected

Many desire to be sent until they realize it means being misunderstood, overlooked, and sometimes resisted. Jesus Himself was rejected:

> **"He came to His own, and His own did not receive Him."**
> **—John 1:11 (NKJV)**

But rejection doesn't mean disqualification. It often confirms that you're walking in the footsteps of the One who sent you.

> **"Blessed are you when they revile and persecute you, and say all kinds of evil against you falsely for My sake." — Matthew 5:11 (NKJV)**

Being sent is not about being liked—it's about being loyal.

Carriers of His Message, Not Ours

When God sends you, you don't carry your own message. You carry His Word. The true sent one is not an opinion-sharer, but a truth-declarer.

> **"Then the Lord put forth His hand and touched my mouth, and the Lord said to me: 'Behold, I have put My words in your mouth.'" —Jeremiah 1:9 (NKJV)**

A sent vessel is entrusted with holy content. This means we must speak only what God speaks, and go only where He sends.

Being Sent Carries the Weight of Heaven's Backing

You are not sent alone. When God sends you, He goes with you.

> **"Have I not commanded you? Be strong and of good courage... for the Lord your God is with you wherever you go." —Joshua 1:9 (NKJV)**

> **"And they went out and preached everywhere, the Lord working with them and confirming the word through the accompanying signs." —Mark 16:20 (NKJV)**

The power is not in the vessel, but in the One who sends. Miracles follow the sent. Deliverance follows the sent. Transformation follows the sent.

The Sent Are Positioned for Kingdom Impact

When Paul and Barnabas were sent by the Holy Spirit (**see Acts 13:2–4**), entire regions were shaken. When Jonah was sent (after being rerouted by disobedience), a whole city repented. When Jesus sent the seventy, demons submitted, and people were healed (**see Luke 10:17**).

You are not sent to fill a church pew—you are sent to shift atmospheres, rescue souls, and declare God's truth.

Being sent gives your life eternal relevance.

Don't Just Go—Be Sent

There is a difference between going and being sent. Going without being sent leads to frustration and burnout, but being sent leads to favor, authority, and kingdom impact. Before you move, pause. Listen. Wait for His voice. When He sends you, He equips you.

"And how shall they preach unless they are sent?" — Romans 10:15 (NKJV)

The church doesn't need more performers. It needs sent ones. And the world is not waiting for another program—it's waiting for the manifestation of the obedient.

Will you wait to be sent? And when He sends you, will you go, no matter the cost?

REFLECTION QUESTIONS

1. Have you ever gone ahead of God instead of waiting to be sent?

2. Are you willing to surrender your comfort, plans, and expectations in order to go where God sends?

3. What message has God placed in your heart that you've been hesitant to carry?

DECLARATION

I will not move unless You send me, Lord. I surrender to Your timing, Your path, and Your purpose. I will not chase platforms—I will wait for Your commission. When You send me, I will go boldly, faithfully, and fearlessly. I am Yours.

CHAPTER 5

DYING TO SELF — THE COST OF THE CALL

To say "Lord, send me" is to say, "Lord, kill everything in me that would hinder Your will." It is not a light or convenient request. It is a cry of surrender that carries with it the weight of death—death to comfort, pride, self-will, and personal ambition. Every person God sends must first pass through the grave of self.

> **"Then Jesus said to His disciples, 'If anyone desires to come after Me, let him deny himself, and take up his cross, and follow Me.'" —Matthew 16:24 (NKJV)**

The call of God demands crucifixion—not a literal one, but the crucifixion of your flesh, ego, and preferences. It is impossible to be fully used by God while still clinging to the control of self.

There Is No Sending Without Surrender

Jesus did not just teach; He laid down His life. Paul did not just preach; he poured out his life as a drink offering (**see Philippians 2:17**). Peter did not just follow; he was willing to be crucified for the name of Jesus. The gospel is not advanced through talent, but through total surrender.

> **"I have been crucified with Christ; it is no longer I who live, but Christ lives in me..." —Galatians 2:20 (NKJV)**

To be sent, you must first die.

— Die to applause.
— Die to being understood.
— Die to controlling the outcome.
— Die to your own version of success.

Only dead men and women can truly carry resurrection power.

Self-Will Is the Enemy of Obedience

One of the most subtle enemies of the call is partial obedience. When self is still on the throne, we obey what is comfortable and resist what is costly. But the Lord does not send half-submitted vessels.

> **"...not My will, but Yours, be done." —Luke 22:42 (NKJV)**

This was not just a moment in the garden for Jesus—it is a model for all who are called. You cannot walk in divine sending while holding on to personal control.

When self is alive:

- You question God's timing.
- You resist uncomfortable assignments.
- You seek validation from people instead of approval from God.

When self is dead:

- You obey without delay.
- You endure hardship without bitterness.
- You pursue the mission, even when misunderstood.

The Altar Is Not Just a Place of Prayer—It's a Place of Death

In the Old Testament, the altar was not for decoration—it was for sacrifice. The fire of God always fell on something that died. If you desire God's fire, you must climb onto the altar.

> **"...present your bodies a living sacrifice, holy, acceptable to God, which is your reasonable service." —Romans 12:1 (NKJV)**

A living sacrifice is one who chooses to stay surrendered daily, even when the flesh wants to crawl off the altar.

The Cost Includes Isolation, Opposition, and Testing

Being sent by God means being willing to endure seasons of:

- **Loneliness** – Elijah stood alone on Mount Carmel.
- **Rejection** – Jeremiah was thrown into a pit for preaching truth.
- **Testing** – Jesus was led by the Spirit into the wilderness before His public ministry (**see Matthew 4:1**).

God proves those He plans to use. The fire is not punishment—it's preparation. You cannot lead others to die to self if you have not been there yourself.

> **"though He was a Son, yet He learned obedience by the things which He suffered." —Hebrews 5:8 (NKJV)**

Obedience is not learned in comfort. It is forged in the furnace.

The Sent Must Lose Their Life to Gain It

Jesus made it clear that following Him would cost everything, but gain eternity.

> **"For whoever desires to save his life will lose it, but whoever loses his life for My sake will find it." —Matthew 16:25 (NKJV)**

To lose your life is not necessarily to die physically, but to give up the right to live according to your own plans, dreams, and desires. It is to trade your story for His mission.

God Sends the Broken, Not the Boastful

Brokenness is not weakness—it is readiness. God resists the proud but gives grace to the humble (**see James 4:6**). Only the truly broken can carry the weight of glory without being crushed by it.

> **"The sacrifices of God are a broken spirit, a broken and a contrite heart—these, O God, You will not despise." — Psalm 51:17 (NKJV)**

Before God sends you to the nations, He often sends you to your knees. Those who carry the greatest anointing are often those who have walked through the greatest breaking.

The Price Is High, But the Reward Is Eternal

There is a cost to the call. It will cost you everything, but give you more than you ever imagined. When you truly die to self, you are free to live for Him. And when you live for Him, you become a vessel of eternal value.

Let these words echo in your spirit:

> *"Lord, not my will, but Yours be done. Let me decrease, so You may increase. Crucify my flesh, silence my pride, and destroy my selfish ambition. I am not my own. I belong to You."*

Only when we die can we be truly sent.

REFLECTION QUESTIONS

1. What areas of your life have you not fully surrendered to God?

2. Are there things you need to die to in order to walk in full obedience?

3. What is the hardest part of the call for you to embrace— and why?

DECLARATION

I die to self. I lay down my desires, my comfort, and my control. I surrender fully to God's will. I embrace the cost of the call, knowing that obedience to Him is worth more than anything this world can offer. I am crucified with Christ, and I live only for His glory.

CHAPTER 6

WHERE HE SENDS, HE PROVIDES

When God sends you, He takes full responsibility for your journey. He does not just call you to go—He equips you for the mission. His provision is not an afterthought—it is tied to His purpose. Where God sends, He always provides.

"And my God shall supply all your need according to His riches in glory by Christ Jesus." —Philippians 4:19 (NKJV)

The One who sends is also the One who sustains. His provision may not always come in the way you expect, but it will always be enough to fulfill what He has assigned you to do.

Provision Follows Obedience

Too often, we ask God to provide before we step out. But the biblical pattern is that provision is released after obedience. When Abraham was told to sacrifice Isaac, he obeyed even when it made no sense. It wasn't until he lifted the knife that God showed him the ram in the thicket (**see Genesis 22:13**).

"And Abraham called the name of the place, The-LORD-Will-Provide..." —Genesis 22:14 (NKJV)

The altar of obedience became the place of supernatural provision.

When God sends you:

- He will give you the resources.
- He will send the helpers.
- He will open the doors.
- He will make a way in the wilderness (**see Isaiah 43:19**).

But often, the provision is waiting on the other side of your yes.

God's Provision May Look Unfamiliar

When God provided for Elijah during the drought, He didn't send money—He sent ravens.

> **"The ravens brought him bread and meat in the morning, and bread and meat in the evening..." —1 Kings 17:6 (NKJV)**

Later, He sent him to a widow in Zarephath (**see 1 Kings 17:9–16**). God's methods are unpredictable, but His provision is consistent.

If you're waiting for God to provide in a specific way, you may miss the provision He's already given. He often uses unlikely people, places, and means to sustain those He has sent.

Provision Includes More Than Finances

We often associate "provision" with money, but God's provision is multi-dimensional:

- **Strength**

**"As your days, so shall your strength be." —
Deuteronomy 33:25b (NKJV)**

He provides supernatural endurance for long seasons.

- **Wisdom**

  **"If any of you lacks wisdom, let him ask of God... and
  it will be given to him." —James 1:5 (NKJV)**

Wisdom is provision for leadership, strategy, and discernment.

- **Divine Connections**

God will align you with people you didn't even know you needed—
like Aaron for Moses (**see Exodus 4:14**) or Barnabas for Paul (**see
Acts 9:27**).

- **Spiritual Gifts**

  **"Having then gifts differing according to the grace that
  is given to us, let us use them..." —Romans 12:6
  (NKJV)**

He equips you with gifts to fulfill your assignment with
supernatural power.

Provision Does Not Eliminate Faith

Even when provision is promised, walking by faith is still required.
God may not give you the full amount—He may give you just

enough for today. This keeps you dependent, humble, and prayerful.

"Give us this day our daily bread." —Matthew 6:11 (NKJV)

When the Israelites were in the wilderness, God gave them manna, one day at a time (**see Exodus 16:4**). Why? To teach them to trust Him daily.

If you're waiting for everything to line up before you move, you may never go. God's provision flows as you walk in faith, not fear.

He Provides According to Purpose, Not Preference

God funds His assignments, not our agendas. If you're walking in divine purpose, you can expect divine backing. But if you're trying to build your own platform, don't expect heaven to sponsor it.

"You ask and do not receive, because you ask amiss, that you may spend it on your pleasures." —James 4:3 (NKJV)

God doesn't provide to make us comfortable—He provides to make us effective.

So ask yourself: *Is what I'm praying for connected to what He sent me to do?*

He Will Sustain You in Dry Seasons

Being sent doesn't mean you won't walk through deserts. But it means you won't die in them. God kept Elijah fed during a famine.

He kept Paul safe in shipwrecks. He sustained Jesus in the wilderness.

"The young lions lack and suffer hunger; but those who seek the Lord shall not lack any good thing." —Psalm 34:10 (NKJV)

Even when you don't feel abundance, you can walk in confidence because the Sender is also the Sustainer.

Your Supply Is in Your Sending

If God sent you, He has already made provision for everything you need to complete the assignment. You are not walking alone. You are not unsupported. You are not forgotten. He is the God who goes before you and makes provision ahead of you.

"The Lord is my shepherd; I shall not want." —Psalm 23:1 (NKJV)

Don't let the fear of lack stop you from saying yes to the call. If God gave you the vision, He will also send the provision. It's not your job to figure it all out—it's your job to follow His voice. Provision always follows obedience.

REFLECTION QUESTIONS

1. Have you been delaying obedience because of fear that God won't provide?

2. In what ways has God already shown His provision in past seasons?

3. Are you trusting more in visible resources or in the Source Himself?

DECLARATION

I believe that where God sends me, He will provide. I do not walk in fear or doubt. I trust in the Lord my Shepherd, and I declare I lack nothing. I walk in obedience, knowing provision is already waiting for me. Jehovah Jireh is my source.

CHAPTER 7

THE FIRE THAT FUELS THE MISSION

No one can be sent by God and remain passive, apathetic, or lukewarm. Those who are truly sent carry fire. This fire is not natural—it is supernatural. It is not stirred by emotion but ignited by the presence of God. It is this fire that sustains the mission, overcomes fear, and keeps the messenger burning when others would quit.

> **"But His word was in my heart like a burning fire shut up in my bones; I was weary of holding it back, and I could not." —Jeremiah 20:9 (NKJV)**

The mission of God requires more than training—it requires fire. Without the fire, you may start—but you won't last.

What Is the Fire of God?

The fire of God represents:

- **His presence**

> **"For the Lord your God is a consuming fire..." — Deuteronomy 4:24 (NKJV)**

- **His holiness**

  "And one cried to another and said: 'Holy, holy, holy is the Lord of hosts...' And the posts of the door were shaken... and the house was filled with smoke." — Isaiah 6:3–4 (NKJV)

- **His power and anointing**

  "Then there appeared to them divided tongues, as of fire, and one sat upon each of them." —Acts 2:3 (NKJV)

- **His passion for souls and justice**

  "For Zion's sake I will not hold My peace, and for Jerusalem's sake I will not rest..." —Isaiah 62:1a (NKJV)

God's fire is not symbolic—it is transformational. When you encounter Him, you don't just get inspired; you get ignited.

The Fire Is Caught at the Altar

Before you are sent out to preach or lead, you must come near to God's altar. The fire doesn't fall in the crowd—it falls on the altar of sacrifice.

> **"and fire came out from before the Lord and consumed the burnt offering..." —Leviticus 9:24 (NKJV)**

You cannot fake fire. You either carry it or you don't. You either burn with God's burden, or you rely on performance. Before Isaiah was sent to prophesy, the fire touched his lips (**see Isaiah 6:6–8**). He was not just given a message—he was set on fire.

The Sent Ones Burn for Souls

Those who are truly sent carry a divine urgency. They cannot rest while people perish. They do not minimize the mission, dilute the message, or delay their movement.

> **"Because zeal for Your house has eaten me up, and the reproaches of those who reproach You have fallen on me."**
> **—Psalm 69:9 (NKJV)**

When the fire of God burns in your heart:

- Your prayer life intensifies.
- Your passion for souls increases.
- Your desire for holiness deepens.
- Your appetite for revival becomes unquenchable.

This fire becomes the fuel of your mission. Without it, ministry becomes mechanical and joyless. With it, even hardship becomes holy.

You Cannot Carry the Fire and Stay Comfortable

Fire disrupts. It burns everything that is not surrendered. It purges the flesh, exposes the heart, and consumes the idols.

> **"He will baptize you with the Holy Spirit and fire."** —
> **Matthew 3:11 (NKJV)**

Those baptized in fire are not satisfied with the status quo Christianity. They disrupt demonic systems, challenge religious complacency, and walk in supernatural boldness. Their lives provoke others to awaken.

Fire-carriers:

- Pray when others sleep.
- Weep when others laugh.
- Go when others stay.

The fire makes them dangerous to hell and unshakable on earth.

The Fire Must Be Tended Daily

Like the priests of old, you must keep the fire burning in your heart.

> **"The fire shall ever be burning upon the altar; it shall never go out." —Leviticus 6:13 (KJV)**

You tend the fire through:

- Consistent prayer.
- Fasting and consecration.
- Meditation on the Word.
- Staying near a godly community.
- Obedience without delay.

Fire dies in cold atmospheres. Surround yourself with those who burn, or you'll slowly grow cold.

Without the Fire, You'll Burn Out

Many people burn out in ministry, not because the work was too much, but because they lacked the fire. You can't run on zeal alone; you need Holy Ghost fire that renews you daily.

> **"Even the youths shall faint and be weary, and the young men shall utterly fall, but those who wait on the Lord shall renew their strength;" —Isaiah 40:30–31a (NKJV)**

The fire of God is not a moment—it is a lifestyle. You don't get it once at an altar—you nurture it daily through intimacy with God.

The Fire Is Your Fuel

You were never meant to fulfill the Great Commission in your own strength. You were meant to be sent in fire, led by fire, and protected by fire—just like Israel in the wilderness (**see Exodus 13:21**).

If you feel weak, dry, or disillusioned, ask for the fire again. He is still the Baptizer. He is still the Consuming Fire. And He is still looking for those who will burn for Him.

> **"Did not our heart burn within us while He talked with us…?" —Luke 24:32 (NKJV)**

Let that be your testimony—a heart that burns.

REFLECTION QUESTIONS

1. Have you lost the fire you once had for God and His mission?

2. What areas of your life need to be placed on the altar again?

3. Are you surrounding yourself with people who feed your fire or smother it?

DECLARATION

Lord, set me on fire again. Let me burn with passion for Your presence and purpose. I refuse to live lukewarm or complacent. I am a fire-carrier, and I will not allow the flame to go out. Ignite me, fuel me, send me.

CHAPTER 8

OVERCOMING THE FEAR OF GOING

F ear is often the invisible wall standing between a willing heart and a world in need. Many say, "Lord, send me"—but freeze when the call requires movement. It's not rebellion. It's not indifference. It's fear. And if fear is not confronted, it will cripple your calling.

"For God has not given us a spirit of fear, but of power and of love and of a sound mind." —2 Timothy 1:7 (NKJV)

You were not created to be ruled by fear. You were created to walk in the authority of heaven. Every person God has ever sent had to overcome fear to walk in faith. So must we.

Fear Often Follows the Call

From Genesis to Revelation, God's call is often followed by a fearful response:

- Moses feared he was unqualified (**see Exodus 3:11**).
- Jeremiah feared he was too young (**see Jeremiah 1:6**).
- Gideon feared he was too weak (**see Judges 6:15**).
- Jonah ran away in fear (**see Jonah 1:3**).

And yet God did not retract His call. He equipped them, empowered them, and patiently pushed them forward.

> **"Do not be afraid of their faces, for I am with you to deliver you," says the Lord. —Jeremiah 1:8 (NKJV)**

God does not minimize our fear—He speaks directly to it. He gives us courage, not through comfort but through His presence.

Types of Fear That Hinder the Called

1. Fear of Failure – "What if I don't succeed?"

Success in the kingdom is measured by obedience, not outcomes.

> **"So then each of us shall give account of himself to God." —Romans 14:12 (NKJV)**

2. Fear of People – "What will they think or say?"

The fear of man is a trap that silences the sent.

> **"The fear of man brings a snare, but whoever trusts in the Lord shall be safe." —Proverbs 29:25 (NKJV)**

3. Fear of Lack – "Will God really provide?"

This fear is crushed by trusting the God of provision (**see Philippians 4:19**).

4. Fear of the Unknown – "What if I don't know what's next?"

Faith requires trusting, even when the path isn't clear.

> **"For we walk by faith, not by sight."** —2 Corinthians 5:7 (NKJV)

Courage Is Not the Absence of Fear—It's the Presence of Faith

Every hero of the Bible felt fear. But they moved forward anyway. That's courage. It's not being fearless—it's being faithful in the face of fear.

> **"Be strong and of good courage; do not be afraid, nor be dismayed, for the Lord your God is with you wherever you go."** —Joshua 1:9 (NKJV)

Joshua had big shoes to fill after Moses, but God gave him courage by reminding him of His presence.

If you know God is with you, you can go anywhere.

Fear Is Often the Indicator of Purpose

Wherever there's great resistance, there's often great assignment. Fear tries to guard the gates of destiny. Satan uses fear as a weapon to intimidate the called because he knows the moment you move, something will shift.

The places you fear to go are often the places where your greatest impact will happen.

"Yea, though I walk through the valley of the shadow of death, I will fear no evil; for You are with me…" —Psalm 23:4 (NKJV)

Practical Ways to Overcome Fear

1. Pray Boldly

Fear flees when faith is fed.

> **"In the day when I cried out, You answered me, and made me bold with strength in my soul."** —Psalm 138:3 (NKJV)

2. Remember Past Victories

Rehearsing God's past faithfulness builds present courage.

3. Stay in the Word

> **"Your word is a lamp to my feet and a light to my path."** —Psalm 119:105 (NKJV)

The Word silences the voice of fear.

4. Speak Faith

What you say affects what you feel. Speak the Word aloud.

5. Take One Step at a Time

You don't have to see the whole staircase—just take the first step.

Your Obedience Sets Others Free

You're not just fighting fear for yourself—you're breaking fear for others. Every "yes" you give to God makes it easier for someone else to say "yes."

When Paul obeyed and went, churches were planted, letters were written, and lives were changed.

> **"I was with you in weakness, in fear, and in much trembling... but in demonstration of the Spirit and of power." —1 Corinthians 2:3–4 (NKJV)**

Fear didn't stop him—and it must not stop you. Your obedience has ripple effects in the kingdom.

Feel the Fear—Then Go Anyway

God never promised you wouldn't feel fear. He promised He would be with you in it. If you wait until you feel ready, you'll wait forever. The secret is this: go while trembling. Obey while afraid. Move while praying. And as you go, God will strengthen you, surround you, and show you that His perfect love casts out all fear (**see 1 John 4:18**).

You are not disqualified because you feel afraid. But you are empowered when you move forward anyway.

> **"Have I not commanded you? Be strong and of good courage..." —Joshua 1:9 (NKJV)**

The mission is too important to be delayed by fear. Let courage rise. Let fear fall.

REFLECTION QUESTIONS

1. What fears have been keeping you from fully walking in your calling?

2. How has fear disguised itself as "wisdom" or "waiting on confirmation" in your life?

3. What truth from God's Word can you stand on today to silence fear?

DECLARATION

Fear will not hold me back. I am called, equipped, and sent by God. I will not fear people, lack, failure, or the unknown. I go in boldness, covered by grace and led by the Spirit. Where God sends me, I will go—without fear, without delay, and without apology.

CHAPTER 9

REACHING THE LOST AT ANY COST

The heartbeat of heaven is souls. The reason God sends, speaks, and saves is because He desires that none should perish. If we say, "Lord, send me," but do not carry His burden for the lost, we have missed the very point of our calling.

"For the Son of Man has come to seek and to save that which was lost." —Luke 19:10 (NKJV)

This is not just Christ's mission—it must be ours. To be truly sent by God is to be gripped by a holy urgency for the salvation of others. Nothing matters more. Reaching the lost isn't a side assignment—it's the main mission.

The Lost Are Not Just Numbers—They Are Souls

It is possible to become so focused on ministry activities that we forget the ultimate purpose: eternal rescue. Every soul matters. Every person who dies without Christ is eternally separated from God.

"And anyone not found written in the Book of Life was cast into the lake of fire." —Revelation 20:15 (NKJV)

This is not fear-based evangelism—it is truth-based compassion. Jesus spoke more about hell than many preachers today. Why? Because He came to save us from it.

If the lost are not your burden, they will never be your priority.

The Gospel Is Good News—But It Must Be Delivered

The gospel is not powerful just because it exists—it is powerful because it is proclaimed.

> **"How then shall they call on Him in whom they have not believed? And how shall they believe in Him of whom they have not heard?" —Romans 10:14 (NKJV)**

The gospel must be spoken, preached, taught, and shared. People do not just find Christ by accident—they find Him when someone brings the message.

You don't have to be a pulpit preacher—you just have to be an obedient witness.

At Any Cost Means:

1. At the Cost of Comfort

Evangelism is rarely convenient. It may involve long conversations, altered schedules, or loving people who are difficult to love.

> **"Go out into the highways and hedges, and compel them to come in, that My house may be filled." —Luke 14:23 (NKJV)**

2. At the Cost of Reputation

Jesus was accused of being a friend of sinners—because He was. Reaching the lost might get you misunderstood by the religious. But pleasing God matters more.

3. At the Cost of Time and Resources

Soul-winning may cost you sleep, money, and time, but what better investment is there than eternity?

4. At the Cost of Rejection

Some will ignore you, mock you, or even oppose you. But the reward of one soul saved outweighs a thousand "no's."

Jesus Modeled Relentless Love

Jesus:

- Went out of His way to reach one woman at a well (**see John 4**).
- Healed a demon-possessed man and sent him to evangelize his region (**see Mark 5**).
- Ate with tax collectors and sinners (**see Matthew 9:10**).

He didn't wait for the lost to come to Him—He went to them. That is the essence of being sent.

Your Testimony Is a Weapon

You may not have all the theological answers, but you have something more powerful—your story.

> **"And they overcame him by the blood of the Lamb and by the word of their testimony…" —Revelation 12:11 (NKJV)**

Share what Jesus has done for you. Someone is waiting to hear how you were delivered, healed, changed, and restored.

Reaching the Lost Requires Spiritual Urgency

You don't have forever to obey. And the lost don't have forever to be reached.

> **"Do you not say, 'There are still four months and then comes the harvest'? Behold, I say to you, lift up your eyes and look at the fields, for they are already white for harvest!" —John 4:35 (NKJV)**

The harvest is now. The time is now. The lost can't wait for a more convenient moment. If you've been sent, go now.

Let the Cost Be Counted—but Let the Mission Be Completed

Jesus said:

> **"…whoever of you does not forsake all that he has cannot be My disciple." —Luke 14:33 (NKJV)**

Reaching the lost will cost you. But the reward is eternal. What price are you willing to pay for someone else's soul to be saved?

Let your life be a living sermon. Let your witness speak louder than your words. Let your obedience lead to someone else's deliverance.

Love Must Lead the Way

Jesus was moved with compassion (**see Matthew 9:36**). And if we are truly sent by Him, we too must be moved—not by duty, but by love.

You are not sent to entertain the saved—you are sent to rescue the perishing. This is the great commission. This is the eternal assignment. This is the mission of heaven.

"...he who wins souls is wise." —Proverbs 11:30 (NKJV)

Will you risk your comfort for someone else's salvation? Will you lay aside your plans to be part of God's rescue mission?

Whatever the cost, reach them.

REFLECTION QUESTIONS

1. How deeply do you feel God's burden for the lost?

2. What fears or hesitations have held you back from sharing the gospel?

3. Who in your life right now is waiting on your obedience?

DECLARATION

Lord, break my heart for the lost. Give me eyes to see the harvest. I will not ignore, delay, or excuse my calling. I will reach the lost at any cost—with love, boldness, and urgency. Let my life be a rescue mission.

CHAPTER 10

THE REWARD OF OBEDIENCE

Obedience to God is never without cost, but it is also never without reward. Every sacrifice, every "yes," every step of faith is seen by God, recorded in eternity, and rewarded both now and in the life to come. Obedience may not always bring immediate applause, but it always brings divine approval.

"If you are willing and obedient, you shall eat the good of the land." —Isaiah 1:19 (NKJV)

The reward of obedience is far greater than any reward this world could offer. The obedient don't just live for earth—they live for the eternal.

Obedience Pleases the Heart of God

Before reward comes, there is relationship. The greatest reward of obedience is intimacy with God. Obedience is an expression of love.

"If you love Me, keep My commandments." —John 14:15 (NKJV)

"...to obey is better than sacrifice..." —1 Samuel 15:22 (NKJV)

When you obey God, you position yourself to walk closely with Him. You become trustworthy in His eyes. You become someone He can use, speak through, and walk with. That is a reward greater than any material blessing.

Obedience Unlocks Supernatural Favor

Throughout scripture, obedience always unlocked God's hand of favor:

- Noah obeyed and built the ark, and his entire family was saved (**see Genesis 6:22**).
- Abraham obeyed and became the father of many nations (**see Genesis 12:1–3**).
- Peter obeyed Jesus' word and caught a net-breaking load of fish (**see Luke 5:5–6**).

"Blessed is the man who fears the Lord, who delights greatly in His commandments." —Psalm 112:1 (NKJV)

The obedient carry the favor of God. Doors open. Provision flows. Miracles manifest. Not because of who they are, but because they simply did what He said.

Obedience Produces Spiritual Authority

You cannot walk in authority if you are not under authority. God entrusts spiritual power to those who are submitted.

"Therefore submit to God. Resist the devil and he will flee from you." —James 4:7 (NKJV)

Submission comes before resistance. When you are obedient to God, the enemy loses power over your life. Your prayers carry weight. Your words carry power. Your presence carries light.

Obedience Impacts Generations

Your obedience is not just about you—it's about those connected to you. Abraham's obedience blessed Isaac, Jacob, and generations afterward. Rahab's obedience to hide the spies spared her family. Your "yes" may set off a chain reaction of deliverance, healing, and revival in your family, church, and city.

"but showing mercy to thousands, to those who love Me and keep My commandments." —Exodus 20:6 (NKJV)

You may never fully see the impact of your obedience on this side of eternity, but heaven is recording every act of faithfulness.

Obedience Qualifies You for Greater Assignments

Jesus said:

"Well done, good and faithful servant; you were faithful over a few things, I will make you ruler over many things." —Matthew 25:21 (NIV)

Obedience in small things positions you for larger influence. God doesn't promote based on popularity—He promotes based on faithfulness.

If you obey when no one sees, He can trust you in public ministry. If you obey when it's hard, He can trust you in moments of spiritual warfare.

Obedience Prepares You for Eternal Reward

There are crowns promised for those who live faithfully and obey Christ. Your obedience is an investment in eternity.

> **"And behold, I am coming quickly, and My reward is with Me, to give to every one according to his work." — Revelation 22:12 (NKJV)**

Heaven is not just about being saved—it's also about being rewarded for what you did with what you were given.

Paul said:

> **"I have fought the good fight, I have finished the race, I have kept the faith. Finally, there is laid up for me the crown of righteousness..." —2 Timothy 4:7–8 (NKJV)**

This is the reward of those who remain faithful, who obey to the end, and who refuse to compromise.

Obedience Is Its Own Reward

Yes, there are blessings, favor, and eternal crowns, but the real reward is walking in step with the will of God. There is peace in obedience. There is joy in surrender. There is clarity in submission.

You don't have to strive—you just have to obey. And in obedience, your purpose unfolds.

"Great peace have those who love Your law, and nothing causes them to stumble." —Psalm 119:165 (NKJV)

Keep Saying Yes

When you say "yes" to God, you are not losing—you are winning in the most eternal way possible. The world may not understand. The crowd may not applaud. But heaven takes notice.

"Well done, good and faithful servant... Enter into the joy of your Lord." —Matthew 25:23 (NKJV)

That is the ultimate reward of obedience—hearing those words from the One who sent you.

Whatever it costs, whatever it takes—obey Him. The reward is worth it.

REFLECTION QUESTIONS

1. Have you obeyed God in the last instruction He gave you, or are you still waiting for confirmation?

2. What areas of delayed obedience have cost you favor or peace?

3. How have you seen God reward your obedience in past seasons?

DECLARATION

Lord, I choose to obey—fully, quickly, and without compromise. I will not delay, debate, or disobey. I trust that what You ask of me is always for my good and for Your glory. I thank You for the reward of obedience—both now and in eternity.

CHAPTER 11

THE GLOBAL MANDATE — BEYOND OUR BORDERS

The call of God is never confined to comfort zones. The mission of Christ was never meant to be local only—it is global in nature, eternal in scope, and urgent in execution. If we are truly saying, "Lord, send me," we must be prepared to go not only across the street but across the world.

"Go therefore and make disciples of all the nations..." — Matthew 28:19 (NKJV)

The Great Commission is not limited by geography, language, culture, or race. It is a global mandate—from heaven, to the church, for the nations.

God's Heart Has Always Been Global

From Genesis to Revelation, we see God's desire to bless all nations:

- In Genesis 12:3, God tells Abraham:

"In you all the families of the earth shall be blessed."

(NKJV).

- In Isaiah 49:6, the Servant of the Lord is called not just for Israel, but:

  "I will also give You as a light to the Gentiles, that You should be My salvation to the ends of the earth." (NKJV).

- Jesus said in Mark 13:10:

  "And the gospel must first be preached to all the nations." (NKJV).

- And in Revelation 7:9, we see the result:

  "A great multitude... of all nations, tribes, peoples, and tongues, standing before the throne..." (NKJV).

God's plan is global. So our vision must be bigger than buildings, budgets, and borders. It must reflect the vast scope of His redemption.

The Gospel Is for Every Nation, Not Just "Our" Nation

There is no "us vs. them" in the kingdom. There is no "domestic vs. foreign" in the eyes of the One who died for the whole world.

"For God so loved the world..." —John 3:16 (NKJV)

If our gospel does not have global reach, it does not fully reflect the heart of God.

Local ministry is essential, but we must not lose sight of the international burden. God sends some to go physically, and others to give, send, pray, and equip. But every believer plays a part in the global mission.

The Mandate to Go Beyond Borders

Jesus made it clear in Acts 1:8:

> **"But you shall receive power when the Holy Spirit has come upon you; and you shall be witnesses to Me in Jerusalem, and in all Judea and Samaria, and to the ends of the earth." (NKJV).**

That's:

- **Jerusalem** — your immediate area.
- **Judea** — your region.
- **Samaria** — the culturally uncomfortable.
- **Ends of the earth** — nations beyond your own.

This is not a step-by-step process—it's a simultaneous assignment. We must reach people here and there, near and far, familiar and foreign.

Barriers to Global Obedience

1. **Comfort — "It's easier to stay where I know."**

But calling always costs comfort.

2. **Fear — "What if it's dangerous?"**

Safety is not the standard—obedience is.

3. Nationalism — "Let's focus on our own country first."

The kingdom of God transcends political boundaries. We are citizens of heaven first (**see Philippians 3:20**).

4. Ignorance — "I didn't know there were unreached people."

Over 3 billion people today have never heard the gospel. That's not just a statistic—it's a crisis.

> **"And how shall they hear without a preacher?" —Romans 10:14 (NKJV)**

God Still Calls People to the Nations

He called:

- Jonah to Nineveh.
- Paul to Gentile cities.
- Philip to a foreign eunuch (**see Acts 8:26–40**).

And today, He still says, "Who will go for Us?"

Not everyone is called to leave their country, but every Christian is called to be globally minded. Whether you go, send, pray, or fund, you have a part in fulfilling the global mission.

You Have What the Nations Need

The nations don't need another program. They need:

- The gospel of Jesus Christ (**see Romans 1:16**).
- The power of the Holy Spirit (**see Acts 1:8**).
- The compassion of Christ (**see Matthew 9:36**).
- The boldness of the sent (**see Acts 4:29**).

God has deposited something in you that is meant to go beyond borders. Don't limit your assignment to your city if God is calling you to the world.

> **"Ask of Me, and I will give You the nations for Your inheritance..." —Psalm 2:8 (NKJV)**

The Church Must Be Globally Engaged

Churches must raise their vision and see beyond the four walls. A church that is not involved in missions is disobedient to the Great Commission. We must:

- Pray for the nations (**see Matthew 9:38**).
- Send missionaries and evangelists (**see Romans 10:15**).
- Give sacrificially to global outreach (**see 2 Corinthians 9:6–8**).
- Train believers for cross-cultural impact (**see Acts 13:1–3**).

God is calling churches not just to grow inward, but to reach outward.

Don't Limit Your Obedience to Your Zip Code

God is not just the God of your region—He is the Lord of all nations. If you truly say, "Lord, send me," then you must be willing to see the world through His eyes. He's calling for those who will carry the gospel to the streets, the cities, and the ends of the earth.

"And this gospel of the kingdom will be preached in all the world as a witness to all the nations, and then the end will come." —Matthew 24:14 (NKJV)

The global mission is the final frontier of obedience. Let your surrender be bigger than your surroundings. Let your vision extend past your borders.

Say yes to God—for the sake of the nations.

REFLECTION QUESTIONS

1. Have you asked God what your role is in reaching the nations?

2. Are you willing to go, give, or send as He leads?

3. What steps can your church or ministry take to obey the global mandate?

DECLARATION

Lord, I say yes, not just to local impact, but to global assignment. I will not limit my obedience to my comfort zone. Send me to the nations, or use me to send others. Give me Your heart for the world. I carry the gospel beyond borders.

CHAPTER 12

LORD, SEND ME — NOW WHAT?

You've said the words. You've surrendered your heart. You've felt the fire of the call and the burden for souls. You've declared, "Lord, send me." But now you ask: What's next? Where do I go? What do I do?

This chapter is for those who are ready but waiting. Willing but wondering. You're not alone. Many called ones have found themselves in the "now what?" stage. But the same God who calls also leads—step by step, door by door, moment by moment.

"The steps of a good man are ordered by the Lord, and He delights in his way." —Psalm 37:23 (NKJV)

Step One: Stay Near the Sender

Before you go out for God, make sure you're continually sitting with God. The power to go comes from intimacy, not ambition.

"Then He appointed twelve, that they might be with Him and that He might send them out to preach." —Mark 3:14 (NKJV)

Jesus didn't send them before being with them. Your time with God is your preparation, your protection, and your compass. Don't rush to the field before you're full of His Spirit.

- Pray daily.
- Meditate on His Word.
- Seek wise, Spirit-filled counsel.
- Wait for clarity, not just open doors.

Step Two: Be Faithful Where You Are

Often, your sending begins right where you are. You may not go to another country—yet. But you're already in a harvest field.

"He who is faithful in what is least is faithful also in much..." —Luke 16:10 (NKJV)

Before Paul was sent to the Gentiles, he preached in synagogues. Before David ruled a kingdom, he served in the field. Before you reach nations, be faithful in:

- Witnessing to your family.
- Serving in your church.
- Reaching your community.
- Loving the overlooked.

Obedience in the present prepares you for the future.

Step Three: Listen for Specific Instructions

God doesn't just give general calls—He gives specific assignments. That clarity often comes through:

- **Prayer and fasting**

  "As they ministered to the Lord and fasted, the Holy Spirit said, 'Now separate to Me Barnabas and Saul for the work to which I have called them.'" —Acts 13:2 (NKJV)

- **Confirmation through leadership**

God often confirms through spiritual mentors and pastors.

- **Supernatural prompting**

Dreams, visions, and divine timing can all play a part.

Don't move because it looks good—move because God said go. When He sends you, the grace will match the assignment.

Step Four: Be Equipped for the Assignment

Being sent does not mean being unprepared. Jesus trained the disciples. Paul studied and was taught. Being equipped shows that you honor the mission.

"Study to shew thyself approved unto God, a workman that needeth not to be ashamed, rightly dividing the word of truth." —2 Timothy 2:15 (KJV)

Get equipped:

- Learn the Word deeply.
- Develop in prayer and discernment.
- Train in evangelism, cross-cultural ministry, or leadership.

- Stay submitted to accountability.

Preparation is not a delay—it is a divine process. You may be ready in passion, but God wants you ready in power and wisdom.

Step Five: Walk Through the Doors He Opens

Eventually, the time will come when God opens a door you could not open yourself. When He does, walk through it with confidence.

"See, I have set before you an open door, and no one can shut it..." —Revelation 3:8 (NKJV)

That door may be:

- A ministry opportunity.
- A missions trip.
- A local outreach.
- A connection to a new region or nation.

Don't hesitate. Don't overthink. Move by faith, not by fear. He will never send you where His presence and provision will not follow.

What If the Door Doesn't Open Immediately?

Sometimes, the waiting season is the training season. God may test your obedience before the opportunity arrives. Delay is not denial—it's preparation. In the waiting, ask:

- *"Lord, what are You developing in me?"*
- *"What assignment is in front of me now?"*
- *"Am I stewarding this season well?"*

Joseph waited. Moses waited. Jesus waited. And when the fullness of time came, they walked into destiny.

The Sent Life Is a Daily Yes

Being sent isn't just about one big moment—it's about a lifestyle. You don't just say "yes" once. You say "yes" every day.

- Yes, when it's inconvenient.
- Yes, when it's uncomfortable.
- Yes, when the assignment shifts.
- Yes, when no one sees but God.

"I die daily." —1 Corinthians 15:31 (NKJV)

"Here am I! Send me." —Isaiah 6:8 (NKJV)

This is the cry of the surrendered. This is the life of the sent.

Step Forward in Faith

Now what? Now, you walk. You pray. You prepare. You listen. And when the time comes, you go.

— You don't need all the answers.
— You don't need the approval of people.
— You don't even need to feel qualified.

You just need to say, "Lord, send me." And then follow Him—wherever He leads.

"Trust in the Lord with all your heart, and lean not on your own understanding; in all your ways acknowledge Him, and He shall direct your paths." —Proverbs 3:5–6 (NKJV)

Now is the time to step into what He has already prepared.

REFLECTION QUESTIONS

1. What practical steps can you take now to align with your sending?

2. Are you faithful where you are, or waiting for a "bigger" assignment?

3. What might God be saying to you about the next phase of your calling?

DECLARATION

I am ready, Lord. I trust Your timing and Your leading. I will not rush, delay, or resist. I say yes again—today, tomorrow, and always. I am Yours. Send me, and I will go.

CHAPTER 13

STAYING FAITHFUL AFTER BEING SENT

Being sent by God is not a one-time act—it's a lifelong commitment. The initial "yes" is powerful, but it is the daily faithfulness after the sending that determines the fruit of your life. Many begin the journey with zeal, but few finish with faithfulness. Heaven doesn't just applaud the start—it rewards the finish.

"Moreover it is required in stewards that one be found faithful." —1 Corinthians 4:2 (NKJV)

The assignment God gives isn't just about going—it's about staying true, staying pure, and staying faithful, no matter what comes.

Faithfulness Is a Fruit of the Spirit

You don't need charisma to be faithful. You need character. The fruit of the Spirit includes faithfulness because your ability to endure depends on your walk with the Spirit.

"But the fruit of the Spirit is love, joy, peace... faithfulness." —Galatians 5:22 (NKJV)

True faithfulness is:

- Consistency when others quit.
- Obedience when it's hard.
- Endurance when it feels unnoticed.

God is not looking for the flashy—He's looking for the faithful.

The Sent Will Be Tested

Every assignment comes with challenges:

- **Delays** — like Joseph in prison.
- **Persecution** — like Paul in chains.
- **Betrayal** — like Jesus with Judas.
- **Opposition** — like Nehemiah on the wall.

But what separates the truly sent is their ability to remain faithful through the fire.

> **"Be faithful until death, and I will give you the crown of life." —Revelation 2:10 (NKJV)**

If God has called you, He has also graced you to endure.

Guarding Against Burnout and Distraction

After being sent, the enemy often shifts his strategy. If he can't stop you from going, he will try to:

- Wear you down.
- Distract you with lesser things.
- Tempt you to compromise.

- Entice you with pride or offense.

That's why Jesus said:

> **"Watch and pray, lest you enter into temptation. The spirit indeed is willing, but the flesh is weak." —Matthew 26:41 (NKJV)**

Stay faithful by:

- Staying in the Word.
- Keeping a vibrant prayer life.
- Surrounding yourself with godly accountability.
- Revisiting your "why" regularly.

Faithfulness in the Mundane Matters

Not every moment in ministry will feel exciting. Some days you'll sow without seeing results. Some seasons will be dry. But God sees every small act of obedience.

> **"And whatever you do, do it heartily, as to the Lord and not to men." —Colossians 3:23 (NKJV)**

— Every prayer prayed.
— Every person discipled.
— Every lesson taught.
— Every soul reached.

It all matters. It all counts. Keep showing up. Keep pouring out.

Stay Aligned With the One Who Sent You

Drifting begins when you stop hearing the voice of the Sender. You must remain connected to His heart to stay aligned with His mission.

"Abide in Me, and I in you... for without Me you can do nothing." —John 15:4–5 (NKJV)

— Abiding keeps your fire lit.
— Abiding keeps your vision clear.
— Abiding keeps your purpose fresh.

You didn't send yourself so don't try to sustain yourself. Let the One who called you also carry you.

God Honors the Faithful

At the end of your journey, you won't be judged by how many followers you had, how many likes you gained, or how famous you became. You will be measured by this:

"Well done, good and faithful servant..." —Matthew 25:21 (NKJV)

That is the ultimate goal. Not being celebrated by man, but being approved by God.

Examples of Faithfulness After the Sending

- Noah preached for decades without converts, but remained obedient.
- Daniel stayed faithful in Babylon, despite cultural pressure.

- Anna the prophetess worshipped daily in the temple, waiting faithfully for the Messiah **(see Luke 2:36–38)**.
- Jesus, the ultimate model, remained faithful all the way to the cross.

"Looking unto Jesus, the author and finisher of our faith…" —Hebrews 12:2 (NKJV)

If He finished well, you can too.

Finish What You Started

You said, "Lord, send me." Now say, "Lord, keep me faithful."

You stepped out in obedience—now walk it out in perseverance.

Don't just be someone who answered the call. Be someone who completed the mission.

"I have fought the good fight, I have finished the race, I have kept the faith." —2 Timothy 4:7 (NKJV)

You were never called to be perfect, but you were called to be faithful. God will sustain you. Heaven is cheering for you. The harvest still needs you.

Stay faithful. Stay focused. Stay sent.

REFLECTION QUESTIONS

1. What are the biggest distractions or temptations that threaten your faithfulness?

2. How can you intentionally remain connected to the voice of the Sender?

3. Have you considered quitting, and what has kept you going?

DECLARATION

Lord, I will remain faithful to what You have called me to do. I will not grow weary. I will not give up. I am not moved by feelings or applause—I am anchored in Your Word and committed to the mission. I will finish strong.

CHAPTER 14

WHEN THE SENT ONES ARE WOUNDED

Being sent by God doesn't make you immune to pain. In fact, those who are sent often experience deeper levels of betrayal, misunderstanding, spiritual warfare, and emotional wounding than they ever imagined. The same hands that say, "Here I am, Lord, send me," may later hold wounds inflicted by the very ones they were sent to reach.

Yet God is not only the One who sends—He is also the One who heals.

"He heals the brokenhearted and binds up their wounds."
—Psalm 147:3 (NKJV)

Wounded warriors are still God's chosen vessels. But the question is not if you'll be wounded—the question is what will you do with the wounds?

Yes, the Sent Can Be Hurt

Consider the Bible's examples:

- Moses was constantly criticized by the very people he delivered (see **Numbers 14:2**).
- David was hunted by Saul, whom he served faithfully (**see 1 Samuel 19:10**).
- Jeremiah was mocked, beaten, and imprisoned for speaking God's word (**see Jeremiah 20:2**).
- Paul was beaten, stoned, and abandoned by former companions (**see 2 Timothy 4:10**).
- Jesus was betrayed, rejected, and crucified by the people He came to save (**see John 1:11**).

Being wounded doesn't disqualify you, but bitterness will. How you handle the wound determines how long you stay in the assignment.

Common Wounds the Sent Suffer

1. **Rejection** — When people you pour into walk away.

2. **Betrayal** — When those closest to you turn on you.

3. **Criticism** — When your obedience is misunderstood.

4. **Loneliness** — When your calling feels isolating.

5. **Exhaustion** — When you serve without reciprocation.

   "For we do not have a High Priest who cannot sympathize with our weaknesses…" —Hebrews 4:15 (NKJV)

Jesus understands. And He heals. You don't have to bleed forever.

Don't Hide the Wound—Bring It to the Healer

Many sent ones keep going with open wounds, pretending they're fine while bleeding internally. But unhealed wounds become infected, and infection spreads—to your attitude, your ministry, and your relationships.

God is not asking you to ignore your pain. He's asking you to bring it to Him.

> **"Come to Me, all you who labor and are heavy laden, and I will give you rest." —Matthew 11:28 (NKJV)**

Healing is not weakness—it is wisdom. It's what enables you to keep going without growing bitter.

Wounded, but Still Useful

God uses wounded vessels not perfect ones.

- Jacob walked with a limp but carried a legacy.
- Peter denied Jesus but preached at Pentecost.
- Paul carried a thorn in his flesh but still advanced the gospel.

> **"My grace is sufficient for you, for My strength is made perfect in weakness." —2 Corinthians 12:9 (NKJV)**

Your pain doesn't disqualify your purpose. Your scar is proof that you survived what was meant to stop you.

Don't Let the Wound Become Your Identity

Be honest, but don't become bitter. Be real, but don't remain stuck. You are more than what happened to you.

"Forget the former things; do not dwell on the past. See, I am doing a new thing..." —Isaiah 43:18–19 (NIV)

Yes, they hurt you. Yes, you were misjudged. But you are still sent. You are still anointed. And God still has work for you to do.

Don't bury your gift under the rubble of your pain.

Let the Wound Produce Compassion, Not Contempt

The danger of unhealed wounds is that they make us resent the people we were sent to reach. But the healed heart says:

- *"I remember what it felt like to be rejected, so I won't reject others."*
- *"I was misunderstood, so I'll be patient with those who don't understand."*
- *"I've bled before, so I'll cover others with grace."*

"Blessed are the merciful, for they shall obtain mercy." — Matthew 5:7 (NKJV)

The wounded healer is often the most effective voice for the broken.

Your Healing May Be Someone Else's Hope

The testimony of your survival becomes the weapon someone else needs. Your scars will speak louder than your sermons.

> "And they overcame him by the blood of the Lamb and by the word of their testimony..." —Revelation 12:11 (NKJV)

God never wastes pain. He redeems it. He uses it. He multiplies it for the sake of others.

Heal and Go Again

The wound may have slowed you down, but don't let it stop you. Let God heal you, restore you, and send you again.

> "But may the God of all grace, who called us to His eternal glory by Christ Jesus, after you have suffered a while, perfect, establish, strengthen, and settle you." —1 Peter 5:10 (NKJV)

You are not disqualified. You are not disowned. You are still called. Still chosen. Still sent.

Take time to heal, but then rise again and walk in your assignment with fresh oil, deeper compassion, and unshakable confidence.

You are wounded, but you are still worthy to go.

REFLECTION QUESTIONS

1. Have you been trying to serve while silently wounded?

2. What steps can you take to bring your pain to God honestly and fully?

3. How has your wound changed the way you see others, and has it made you more bitter or more compassionate?

DECLARATION

Lord, I bring my wounds to You. I refuse to hide, numb, or deny my pain. Heal me so I can serve again. Restore my joy, renew my fire, and give me the strength to go again. I am wounded but I am still called. I will rise in grace and walk in obedience.

CHAPTER 15

FINISHING THE ASSIGNMENT

Saying "yes" to God is powerful. Starting the journey is honorable. But finishing the assignment—that is what brings heaven glory and legacy to the earth. Anyone can begin with excitement, but it is those who persevere to the finish who make the most lasting impact.

"But he who endures to the end shall be saved." —Matthew 24:13 (NKJV)

God doesn't just want to send you—He wants you to finish strong. Not limping to the end with regret, but crossing the finish line with fire, faithfulness, and fruit.

The Call Is Not Complete Until the Assignment Is Finished

Jesus declared these words on the cross:

"It is finished." —John 19:30 (NKJV)

He didn't just come to start a movement. He came to complete redemption. Likewise, Paul echoed this in the closing season of his life:

"I have fought the good fight, I have finished the race, I have kept the faith." —**2 Timothy 4:7 (NKJV)**

These were not just poetic words—they were the words of a man who had faced beatings, betrayal, shipwrecks, false accusations, and abandonment—yet stayed the course.

The true test of being sent is not how loudly you start—it's how faithfully you finish.

Why Do So Many Quit Before Finishing?

1. Disappointment with the process.

They thought it would be easier. When trials come, they stop.

2. Discouragement from a lack of results.

They don't see fruit fast enough, so they grow weary.

3. Distraction by lesser assignments.

The enemy tempts them with side paths that feel easier or more glamorous.

4. Disobedience through compromise.

Sin, pride, or spiritual drift leads them off course.

"You ran well. Who hindered you from obeying the truth?" —**Galatians 5:7 (NKJV)**

Finishing requires focus. If you're going to finish, you must keep your eyes on the One who sent you and the purpose that carries eternal weight.

Finishing Requires Grit and Grace

You will not finish the race by passion alone. You need:

- Grit to push through dry seasons.
- Grace to rise when you fall.
- Vision to keep the end in mind.
- Discipline to stay the course.
- Community to help you along the way.
- Holy Spirit power to sustain you.

> **"…let us run with endurance the race that is set before us, looking unto Jesus, the author and finisher of our faith…"**
> **—Hebrews 12:1–2 (NKJV)**

Finishing is not about speed—it's about consistency. It's not about fame—it's about faithfulness. You don't have to impress men. You just have to please the One who called you.

How to Stay Faithful to the Finish

1. Revisit the original call often.

When you're tired or discouraged, remember why you started.

2. Stay rooted in God's Word.

The Word keeps your spirit nourished and your direction clear.

3. Guard against spiritual burnout.

Rest when needed. Take a sabbath. Refuel in God's presence.

4. Stay connected to purpose-driven people.

Isolation is dangerous. Surround yourself with other sent ones.

5. Finish what you start.

If God called you to it, don't quit it. He's not done, and neither are you.

> **"being confident of this very thing, that He who has begun a good work in you will complete it..." —Philippians 1:6 (NKJV)**

God finishes what He starts—and He wants to finish it through you.

Heaven Is Watching the Finish Line

One day, this life will be over. Titles will fade. Accomplishments will pass. But what will matter most is this: *Did I finish my assignment?*

> **"each one's work will become clear... and the fire will test each one's work, of what sort it is." —1 Corinthians 3:13 (NKJV)**

This is not about perfection. It's about perseverance. It's about showing up—again and again—even when it's hard, unnoticed, or painful.

There is a crown for the faithful. There is a reward for the finishers. There is a celebration in heaven for those who endure.

"Blessed is that servant whom his master, when he comes, will find so doing." —Matthew 24:46 (NKJV)

Run Until It's Done

You said, "Lord, send me." And He did. Now, run your race. Stay the course. Endure the process. Refuse to quit. Heaven is waiting— not for those who started with fire, but for those who finish with faith.

Let these be your final words at the end of this journey:

"I have finished the work which You have given Me to do." —John 17:4b (NKJV)

You were called. You were sent. Now, finish the assignment.

REFLECTION QUESTIONS

1. Are there areas of your calling you've left unfinished out of fear, fatigue, or discouragement?

2. What disciplines do you need to strengthen to stay faithful to the end?

3. Are you keeping your eyes on the eternal reward, or have you become distracted?

DECLARATION

Lord, I commit to finishing what You started in me. I will not quit. I will not retreat. I will not grow weary in well-doing. I fix my eyes on Jesus and run the race with endurance. I will finish the assignment and bring You glory.

PROPHETIC CHARGE

ARISE, GO, AND FINISH THE WORK

To every yielded vessel, to every burning heart, to every surrendered soul who has whispered or wept the words, "Lord, send me"—this is your prophetic charge.

You were not born by accident. You were not saved to sit still. You were not called to remain comfortable. Heaven placed eternity in your spirit, and God wrote an assignment across your life. You were marked for movement. You were chosen for impact. You were formed for such a time as this.

> **"Before I formed you in the womb I knew you; before you were born I sanctified you; I ordained you a prophet to the nations." —Jeremiah 1:5 (NKJV)**

God knew your flaws, your fears, your failures—and still He called you. He is not asking for your perfection; He's asking for your obedience. He is not looking for the famous; He's looking for the faithful.

The Trumpet Has Sounded

The trumpet of the Lord is sounding across the earth—not just in cathedrals or crusades, but in living rooms, workplaces, communities, and quiet hearts. The harvest is ripe. The hour is urgent. The time for delay is over.

> **"Arise, shine; for your light has come! And the glory of the Lord is risen upon you." —Isaiah 60:1 (NKJV)**

You are the light. You are the answer someone is praying for. You are the vessel that carries His fire.

You Are Being Sent—But Not Alone

You are not going in your name, your strength, or your reputation. You are going in the power of the Holy Ghost. You are clothed in fire. You are backed by heaven. Angels are being dispatched to walk with you, war for you, and protect the word in your mouth.

> **"Do not be afraid of their faces, for I am with you to deliver you," says the Lord. —Jeremiah 1:8 (NKJV)**

The anointing upon you will break yokes. The word in your mouth will shift atmospheres. The love in your heart will soften hardened souls. And the power within you will point the broken to the only One who saves—Jesus Christ.

Do Not Hold Back

Now is not the time to shrink. Now is not the time to settle. Now is not the time to second-guess your assignment.

> **"Cry aloud, spare not; lift up your voice like a trumpet..." —Isaiah 58:1 (NKJV)**

Preach with boldness. Serve with love. Go with fire. Lay hands on the sick. Proclaim the gospel to the lost. Rebuke compromise. Call forth revival. Win the lost at any cost. Do not be ashamed of the gospel—it is the power of God unto salvation.

Let the Church Arise

Let this charge not rest solely on individuals, but on the church corporately. Let leaders awaken from slumber. Let pulpits burn again. Let disciples be made, not just members gathered. Let soul-winning return to the forefront. Let every ministry return to its mission.

"Go therefore and make disciples of all nations..." — **Matthew 28:19 (NKJV)**

This is our mandate. This is our moment. This is our mission.

Heaven Is Watching. Hell Is Shaking. The Earth Is Waiting.

So arise, sent one. Arise, called one. Arise, burning one.

Walk in what He has spoken.

Go where He is sending.

Finish what He has assigned.

There is a generation waiting for your obedience.

There is a family waiting for your faith.

There is a city waiting for your voice.

There is a nation waiting for your yes.

"For the earnest expectation of the creation eagerly waits for the revealing of the sons of God." —Romans 8:19 (NKJV)

You are not invisible. You are not unimportant. You are a sent one, and your steps are ordered by the Lord.

Now go. With fire. With truth. With urgency. With tears. With the gospel of the kingdom and the power of the Holy Spirit.

Go—and don't come back empty-handed.

DECLARATION

Lord, I receive this charge. I arise in faith, boldness, and obedience. I am sent by the King of kings and I will not delay. I will not hold back. I will run, I will preach, I will go. Use me for Your glory. Let souls be saved, lives be changed, and Your name be made great through my life. In Jesus' name. Amen.

SCRIPTURE REFERENCES BY THEME

The Call of God

- Isaiah 6:8
- Matthew 28:19–20
- John 20:21
- Romans 11:29
- Jeremiah 1:5

Willingness and Surrender

- 2 Timothy 2:21
- Romans 12:1
- Isaiah 1:19
- Luke 9:23
- Proverbs 3:5–6

Hearing the Voice of God

- John 10:27
- Jeremiah 33:3
- Psalm 46:10
- Hebrews 3:15
- Proverbs 4:20–21

Obedience and Faithfulness

- 1 Samuel 15:22

- Deuteronomy 28:1
- James 1:22
- Revelation 2:10
- 1 Corinthians 4:2

Fear and Boldness

- 2 Timothy 1:7
- Joshua 1:9
- Psalm 23:4
- Proverbs 29:25
- Acts 4:29

Provision and Trust

- Philippians 4:19
- Genesis 22:14
- Psalm 23:1
- Deuteronomy 2:7
- Matthew 6:11

Fire and Passion for the Mission

- Jeremiah 20:9
- Acts 2:3
- Leviticus 6:13
- Isaiah 62:1
- Psalm 69:9

Evangelism and the Lost

- Luke 19:10
- Romans 10:14–15
- Matthew 9:37–38
- Proverbs 11:30
- John 4:35

Endurance and Finishing Strong

- 2 Timothy 4:7
- Hebrews 12:1–2
- Revelation 3:11
- Galatians 6:9
- Philippians 1:6

Global Mission and the Nations

- Matthew 28:19
- Acts 1:8
- Revelation 7:9
- Psalm 2:8
- Mark 13:10

www.ingramcontent.com/pod-product-compliance
Lightning Source LLC
LaVergne TN
LVHW021537080426
835509LV00019B/2701